Laugh Yourself Sober
A Zen Way to Sobriety

Broccoli Al

2007

Copyright © 2007 Broccoli Al
All rights reserved.
ISBN: 1-4196-8194-X
ISBN-13: 978-1419681943

Laugh Yourself Sober

TABLE OF CONTENTS

CHAPTER PAGE

1 Welcome to my Zen World	1
2 Some Kind of Alcoholic	7
3 A Temporary Epiphany	25
4 I Finally Get IT Zenwise	33
5 The Zen Way I Came to Belief	43
6 At Last I let God Take Over	55
7 Where Am I, Anyway?	63
8 Why Should I Tell You	67
9 Slippers Monotonous	73
10 Take This Away From Me	79
11 Loaves And Fishes	87
12 I Claim the Right to Be Wrong	93
13 Meditation, The Way To God	97
14 We Awaken and Pay the Bill	103

15 'Tis the Season to Be Sorry	111
16 Three Kinds of Weird Alcoholics	117
17 Fun, Fun, Fun	123
18 Why Can't We All Just Get Along?	131
19 Try To Explain the Unexplainable	137
20 Chippies	143
21 People Don't Act Right	147
Epilogue	151

PREFACE

No matter what hardship he's going through any alcoholic can be "happy, joyous and free."

When I call my friend Daytona Doug, I get a recorded message that says, "I can't come to the phone right now, I'm off somewhere living my dream."

Isn't that marvelous? There may be happier men in this world, but I haven't met them.

If this little book helps bring that kind of happiness to just one person, then it has been worth my while writing it. If it doesn't, that's OK too, because I have enjoyed writing it.

This book is gratefully dedicated to these people who have helped and inspired me in my sobriety:

Bill E. Macon, Ga.

Matt H. Macon, Ga.

"Daytona" Doug G. Daytona beach, Fla.

Arch S. Merritt Island, Fla.

Matthew M. Satellite Beach, Fla.

"Cosmic" Bill P. Melbourne, Fla.

Chapter 1

Welcome to My Zen World

Welcome to my world of Zen, where no matter what happens, alcoholics laugh a lot, live in the now, and just stay out of the way while God works his wonders.

True Zen is an offshoot of Buddhism. Now, I am not a Buddhist. And not being one, I do not believe in reincarnation. If I did I would probably want to come back as a tanning table. Although, with my luck I'd probably wind up in a bathhouse in San Francisco.

But, there are Zen ways of looking at ourselves and the world, that have enormously enhanced our search for serenity and happiness The purpose of this book is to share that with you.

The first Zen story I ever heard was of a Zen master who was being chased by a man-eating tiger. The tiger chased him over a cliff and as he was falling, he grabbed a vine and held on tight. He looked down and saw another man-eating tiger, looking up at him, circling and waiting for him to fall. He looked up and saw two mice gnawing on the vine. He looked to his right and saw a strawberry growing out of the side of the cliff. He plucked the strawberry and ate it. And it tasted so sweet.

And that's the end of the story.

Do you get it?

Do you?

He knew he was going to fall. He knew the tiger below was going to tear him apart. Why should that keep him from enjoying his strawberry?

All my life I have allowed the tigers to keep me from enjoying my strawberries! And as I look back, I see that most of the tigers weren't even real.

I have heard many an alcoholic share in a meeting that he or she was suffering. And yet as I looked around the room, I could see that there was absolutely nothing going on that would cause anyone to suffer. So, that means the sufferer was not here and now in the meeting. The sufferer was somewhere else, in another time and another place.

I believe that is one of the main insanity's of alcoholism.

How many times have we heard new comers share in meetings about suffering over some future court date. The court date will occur only once, but the sufferer was going to court many, many times before then. Doesn't it seem like once is enough?

To me, the Zen I refer to is about living in the now. I don't want to live in the future because I really don't know what's there. And I believe that the reason God put the past in the past is because that's where it belongs. I suspect that God may have invented time and space just to keep everything from happening all at once in the same place.

If you are new to sobriety I envy you. You are at the start of a marvelous adventure into the discovery of a new freedom and a new happiness.

ONE TODAY IS WORTH

TWO TOMORROWS.

BEN FRANKLIN

Chapter 2

Some Kind of Alcoholic

I always introduce myself in meetings by saying, "My name is Al and I'm some kind of alcoholic." I do that because for years people would ask me, "What are you, some kind of alcoholic?" I would always deny it and so that's my acceptance today.

Using the time tested formula of what it was like, what happened and what it's like now, it's necessary that I bore you with my "story."

I was born in 1937, the son of a career Army officer. I spent my early childhood in Oak Ridge, Tennessee during World War II where my father was prominent in founding the Manhattan District Project, better known as the atomic bomb project.

Everything was so secret that my father was never able to share with us what he did for a living. He would only say, "I shuffle papers and write memos to the guy down the hall."

I didn't see much of him because he worked day and night as did everyone else there. After all, there was a war on.

We knew it had something to do with the war, but we didn't know what until the first atomic bomb was dropped on Japan.

We stayed on in Oak Ridge for two more years after the war until my father was transferred to The Armed Forces Staff College in Norfolk, Virginia.

The college itself was a military base operated by The U. S. Marine Corp. in a Navy Town. My little brother and I would take the bus on Saturdays to go to the movies. And the bus was always loaded with sailors.

One day one of the Marines got on the bus with us and the sailors went nuts! They were whistling and yelling things like, "We're safe now, the Marines are here."

At the very next stop, another Marine boarded the bus and the first Marine jumped up and yelled, "Alright, you bastards, now you're out numbered!"

The last time I saw my father I was ten years old. A colonel bucking for promotion to brigadier general, he was transferred from Norfolk to Guam Island in the Pacific Ocean. While he was there the Korean war broke out. He led five battalions into South Korea and died there without ever getting the promotion.

At the time of his transfer to Guam my mother, my little brother and I moved into my grandmother's large house in Rockledge, Florida where she and her two sisters already lived. So from then on I was raised by four widows who would do the best they could with what they had to raise me and teach me how to be a man. They, of course had no idea how to do that.

I see now, looking back on it, that they led fear based lives and they always made fear based decisions because that's the way they were raised.

This meant that anything I wanted to do was brought to a vote. Each one had a veto power so that if the vote was three yes's to one no, the answer was no. That included sports and other after school activities, as well as fishing or hunting trips with school friends of mine and their fathers. Although we lived on the river, boating was out of the question.

The family friends (mostly other old ladies) would often remark on what a gentleman I was and how well adjusted I was. I was well adjusted alright. But, adjusted to what?

With the exception of school nearly everyone I knew was an older adult. My grandmother was a frequent entertainer of the "Girls" of the garden club, The Daughters of the American Revolution, her church circle, etc., etc. And I was nearly always "invited" to help and to be paraded for the approval of those in attendance. I was the mascot.

Three times a day I would pull out four chairs to seat the ladies before I sat down to eat. Whenever we went anywhere I would open four car doors and seat the ladies before we left and do the same thing on the way back and for every stop that was made.

Oddly enough, I was required to always carry a pocket knife and a handkerchief because a lady might need one. Today, a kid would get thrown out of school for having a pocket knife. I never asked why a lady wouldn't carry those things for herself since I had little if any use for either one of them.

That, and going to school on the bus was pretty much my life because there was nobody my age within miles of the house. Summer vacation was a real drag because I almost never even saw anyone my own age the whole time.

While I was still a young child the highlight of my life was the Saturday matinee movies. In those days they had a double feature, cartoons and a serial for kids at the local movie theater.

Parents would drop off their kids for the whole afternoon while they did their shopping or whatever.

Usually the films were cowboy movies. Some would even take their cap pistols to shoot at the bad guys. And although the cowboy movies were the most popular, I preferred the sword fighting pictures.

My friends heroes were Hopalong Cassidy, Gene Autry, and Roy Rogers. My heroes were David Niven and Errol Flynn.

In the sword fighting movies the plot was nearly always the same. The king was dying or off at the crusades and not expected to return. He had two sons. One was the good son and the other son was a drunk. The hero wanted the good son to become king while the prime minister wanted the drunken son to become king so he could be the power behind the throne. The prime minister always had a goatee and wore black leotards.

In the final scene, there was always a pitched battle in the castle. Men were fighting with swords, spears and axes. That is, all but the drunk son. He was standing in the middle of it all, totally oblivious, pouring himself another one. I can remember thinking, "now that's serenity." I didn't want to kill anybody and I certainly didn't care anything about being a king. Here I was, a young child, years before I ever had a drink and the only character in the movie I related to was the only alcoholic in the movie.

After the movie I would buy a bottle of grape soda pop, pretend it was wine, and play out the movie at home with me as the drunken son. How sick is that?

I guess I was already an alcoholic.

I can't tell you how many times I heard my mother say, "Don't do this and don't do that because this is not our house. This is your grandmother's house."

My friends at school called me Butch, which I had taught them to do because I hated my name as well as everything else about myself. One day one of my friends said, "Let's go over to Butch's house."

And I said, "We can't because I don't have one."

I was not a particularly good student, just not very motivated. So my mother thought we could solve that and the problem of the lack of adult male guidance by sending me to military school for my last two years of high school.

But, in military school there was no adult male guidance. Supervision came from other students who out ranked each other. And in my second year I was a sergeant, so I was one of the supervisors!

The following fall I enrolled in the University of Florida where I made three discoveries: freedom, alcohol and the love of my life.

The beautiful girl maintained a 3.0 or better grade point average while I majored in fraternity and flunked out three times. It would be fair to say that I drank my way in and out of college.

I was totally unprepared to handle the freedom or the alcohol. The drinking and partying left little time for unimportant things like classes. My fraternity brothers even warned my girlfriend not to get too involved with me on account of my drinking, but she stood by me anyway.

But, I was COOL! At parties, while the other members of the fraternity were drinking draft beer from the keg provided for that purpose I was drinking cocktails and highballs, which I mixed myself. I thought the others to be much less sophisticated and mature than myself.

Amazingly, when the pretty lady graduated, she married me, much to the dismay of her father who told me, "You're not exactly what we had in mind for our daughter."

We quickly had a child on the way and I knew it was time to settle down and act like a grown-up. I pretty much limited my drinking to weekends and went to work at Cape Canaveral.

I also enrolled in night classes at the Brevard Engineering College, which later became Florida Institute of Technology. I majored in Applied Mathematics and made mostly A's and B's. I pretty much drank on weekends only.

I went to work for Pan American Airways security at the south gate to the Cape where I checked clearances and issued appropriate badges. I worked harder than the others and was hired away by Lockheed Missiles and Space Company on the Polaris program as a blueprint clerk. It was the lowest paid job they had, but it still paid more than the one at Pan American.

Ninety days later I was promoted to Staff Assistant to the Manager of the Engineering Department.

All of this came about as the result of the cunning of the alcoholic mind. I had no idea what was going on, but I could act like I did.

It was less than a week after my promotion. I was at my desk during the noon lunch hour when the phone rang. There was a gruff voice on the line demanding to know the answers to technical questions about anomalies occurring on the missile. I had no idea what he was talking about, so I told him he would have to call back.

He didn't like that at all and said, "By God, do you know who this is? This is (name withheld), Executive Vice President of Lockheed Missiles and Space Company."

So, I said, "By God, do you know who this is?"

"No."

I said, "Good." And I hung up.

I learned later that he was delighted with that and called the Base Manager and said, "If you can find out who that guy is, keep an eye on him. He's a comer!"

There was a public address system which was used to contact people who were not at their desks and every one on the facility would hear it. That sounded like free advertising to me. So I began calling myself. The company receptionist would take the calls from me. And not knowing who it was on the phone, she would page me with lots of phone calls, most of them long distance, and very important sounding. I was getting calls from Sunnyvale, California and the Pentagon in Washington.

About a year later I was promoted to Staff Assistant to the Base Manager. All of this was in an organization of more than 550 engineers, technicians and support personnel.

I picked up on words and used them with out even knowing what they meant. To this day I don't know what a transponder is, but we had a lot of them. We had trouble keeping track of them so I made it my business to know where each and every one was. There is a great deal of power in being the only one who knows.

One day there was a missile ready to be moved to the launch pad and fired. The base manager was not available and there appeared to be a problem. One of the engineers called me and said, "There's too many kilowatts in the jammafram (or something like that), what should we do?"

I didn't have a clue what he was talking about, but it sounded serious. I thought I was busted. I said, "I don't know Clyde. What do you think we should do?"

And he told me!

Of course, I didn't understand a word of what he was saying. So, I quite honestly said, "I don't see anything wrong with that!"

It turned out to be the right thing to do. I took credit for the decision and received a commendation.

All of this was happening and the drinking worsening at the same time. Another thing was growing as well, my ego. I began to believe that I was God's gift to the world of industry.

Before another year had passed two business men suggested that I might be interested heading up a company which would take a franchise for the State of Alabama to market a national business correspondence course. I was to be president of the company, which I thought was a title befitting my abilities.

We began the company in Florence, a small town in northwest Alabama where we could work out, through trial and error the best sales and marketing schemes at minimal expense. Unknown to my investors it had the additional advantage of being in a dry county. And that would solve my drinking problem.

When the little weekly newspaper came out my picture was on the front page with a caption that read, "Former Space Official Moves to Town."

I have no idea what a "Space Official" is. But I liked that title, too.

I was invited to address the Chamber of Commerce. I had no experience with public speaking and I was really nervous. So I drove to Huntsville and back to buy a bottle of courage. I pulled up in front of the Holiday Inn where the meeting was being held, quickly drank the whole bottle down and walked into the meeting cold sober.

I got through the speech O.K. in spite of the fact that I was drunk by the time it ended. I sat down to polite applause and then the idiot running the meeting opened it up for questions!

The first question was, "What should we do if a Soviet missile was headed right for us?"

I couldn't imagine Russian generals sitting around the Kremlin war room, trying to figure out how to get a missile there. Thinking we're probably not being a prime military target I said, "I would call the Chamber of Commerce because they have successfully repelled every thing that's been headed this way for the last thirty years."

I was not invited back and I was not invited to join the Chamber.

Then, under my able direction the company went broke.

I looked in the classified section of the weekly newspaper. There were no openings for space officials.

We moved to Birmingham as the drinking continued to worsen. I landed a job as a salesman with the local Dale Carnegie franchise. One day I was assigned to be a committee member on a committee planing a spring festival parade for the Chamber of Commerce. They obviously had not heard of the previous Chamber of Commerce incident. The result was about the same, except that I told them we were going to get all the virgins in town in the parade but one of them got sick and the other one refused to march by herself.

I finally went to work for a company which was a sales consultant to member firms of the New York Stock Exchange.

We trained stock and bond brokers, mutual fund salesmen and investment bankers in salesmanship.

One night while I was working in Manhattan I was in a Wall Street area bar talking to a great big biker. I have no idea why he was there. I was dressed in a three piece suit and he was wearing his full colors.

We left the bar together, I don't recall where we were going. But, while we were standing there talking, two black and white police cars pulled up. Police officers jumped out of their cars and beat the daylights out of the biker, threw him into a big black paddy wagon and drove off with him.

They put me in the back of a police car and drove me back to my hotel. I wore suits from then on, even for several years after I retired.

I was having more and more difficulty just showing up when and where I was supposed to because of being drunk or on a hangover. But, I must have been pretty good because I began to be asked to speak at sales conventions.

The pay was wonderful (in fact the more you charged them, the better they liked it) and the work was usually for only one hour on any given day. That worked well until I was unable to sufficiently sober up for a speech to a state life insurance convention in an auditorium of more than twenty five hundred salesmen and I passed out in the middle of it.

That career ended immediately and there I was, unemployed again.

I had by this time moved back to Florida.

Well, déjà vu, two prospective business men who thought I knew something about corporate finance because of my association with investment firms, invited me to start a corporation with them. I would be President of it with stock in the venture. I readily agreed and got everything set up, only to get drunk before it really got off the ground. The others had no choice but to buy me out.

Just repeat the above paragraph because it quickly happened again, exactly the same but with different investors!

Then the word got around that we can get Al to start a business, he'll get drunk and we can buy him out. I was the only one who didn't know that.

Another investor came to me with the stupidest idea I had ever seen. But I needed the money so I said, "That sounds like a winner to me!" I'm certainly not proud of it because it was at that moment I became a professional con artist. And I discovered that the world was full of guys who wanted to "give" me money and I was certainly prepared to encourage them to do just that.

Of course, all this time my drinking was progressing. My wife and I were separated many times, but I always took her back. Because I'm good that way.

Bizarre things were beginning to happen. Once, in the middle of the night, I was watching television, drinking a beer when a man I had never seen before came walking out of my bedroom. He asked, "Who the hell are you."

I said, "I'm the home owner here."

He said, "No I'm the homeowner here."

I said, "Well, I'm calling the police!"

He said, "Be my guest."

When the police arrived it turned out that he was right, it was his house. I'm lucky to be alive, I was drinking his beer!

The nice officer took me to the police station and told me I needed help. I remember thinking, "For what?"

He told me that if I sat or lay on a bench there in the station and called somewhere in the morning for help, he wouldn't book me.

I certainly wasn't going to argue with that! In the morning I found a listing in the phone book for Alcoholism Information." I called and asked, "Is this information you have for or about alcoholics?" And the guy on the phone said, "Come on down."

It was a mental health center which today no longer exists. They knew only a little about alcoholism at that time, but bless their hearts, they were trying. They gave me a battery of tests for personality, IQ, etc.

Then they put me in a room with two ladies who called themselves psychiatric nurses. I have no idea what a psychiatric nurse is, but in the movie "One Flew Over the Cuckoo Nest", Nurse Ratchet was one. One was so pretty a man would have to psyche up just to talk to her. If you walked up on her accidentally you would probably just make squeaking noises. The other was seriously obese. Some how as I suspected, the fat one did most of the talking.

I asked, "What did the tests show?" And the fat one said, "You're an Alcoholic, now tell us about your sex problems."

You see, they into Freud. They thought Alcoholism was a psychiatric disorder rather than the primary disease that it is.

I told her I didn't have any sex problems, but she insisted, "You must have, you're an alcoholic."

I explained, "I don't have to dress up in rubber suits, handcuffs, feathers or any of that kind of stuff. And I don't like to do anything hurtful."

She was not satisfied with that, and I was trying to cooperate, so I said, "When I'm drunk, I can't and don't care."

That did not satisfy her and she was so persistent about it that I did a very alcoholic thing.

Have you ever turned an interview around to where you can't tell who's doing the interviewing and who's being interviewed? I said, "You are projecting your sex problems off on me."

She asked, "What do you mean?"

"You must have sex problems or you wouldn't ingest as much food as you do." (See how dishonest I was? I was telling her the truth and I thought I was lying!)

"If that's not caused by sex problems it would have to cause them."

"Unless your husband likes that in which case he has some serious sex problems."

The interview was terminated at that time.

What is really ironic about all this is that I was almost as fat as that poor psychiatric nurse. I couldn't lie down on the beach for fear people would try to push me back in the water.

Later on, after I had joined AA, I went to Overeaters Anonymous and lost seventy seven pounds. It was the easiest thing I had ever done because I was already living the steps. Very quickly I had so many darts taken in my underwear, they just said, "Fruit."

But, I digress.

I went outside and called my wife. I told her I was at the mental health center talking to them about my drinking. She was delighted and told me to wait right there. She was coming to get me.

As she drove up to the center she had a big smile on her face. And I remember thinking, "Wow, these psychiatric nurses really have something."

When I got in the car she asked me what they had said. I told her they said I was an alcoholic. She was delighted with that too, because now we had a name for what was wrong.

She asked, "What else did they say?"

"They told me alcoholism is a disease." (That was about the only thing they had right.)

She was glad to hear that.

I told her, "They said an alcoholic doesn't drink because he wants to, he drinks because has to."

She was pleased with that, too. And so was I. So I told her, "If you had a disease, I would go to the store and buy medicine for you." And I sent her to the package store to buy booze for me.

That didn't last long, because she soon joined a whole coven of black belt Alanons. I don't think they're covens any more, but I sure did then. (Alanon is the spouses of souses.)

I came home in the wee hours one night to find literature on the coffee table. There was a Big Book, a Twelve & Twelve, pamphlets "Twenty Questions" and "A Merry-Go-Round Called Denial". To give you some idea of just how cunning and baffling alcohol is, I remember thinking, "Oh my God! I didn't even know she drank! I can help her."

THE DIFFERENCE BETWEEN
INTELLIGENCE AND STUPIDITY
IS THAT THERE IS A LIMIT
TO INTELLIGENCE.

JORDAN G.

Chapter 3

A Temporary Epiphany

One day I had that "moment of clarity" and thought that I might actually have a drinking problem. So I called a friend of mine I knew who was a member of Alcoholics Anonymous and asked him if I could attend a meeting with him.

I said, "You know that organization you belong to? Well, I think that sounds really interesting. Do you suppose they would mind if I sat in on one of their meetings? I would just monitor it because after all, my interest is merely academic."

He said, "I think that would be fine. There's a meeting tonight at 8 o'clock. I'll pick you up at 7:30. Do you think you can stay away from a drink between now and then?"

I took some offence to that last remark but I said I would.

It was a high bottom group, meeting in a church. There were so many Cadillacs and Lincolns in the parking lot it looked more like a Texas PTA meeting than what I thought an AA meeting would be. That was the craziest bunch of people I ever saw. They were smoking cigarettes and drinking coffee and I think some of them were smoking coffee and drinking cigarettes.

They kept saying, "It's the first drink that gets you drunk."

And I remember thinking, "No wonder these people have to go to all those meetings if they can't drink any better than that. You can't take them anywhere."

The thing that bothered me most was a feeling of betrayal! They had obviously held conferences with my wife and she had told them everything I had been doing, and exactly what to say. How else could they have known?

I know that many people cannot remember their first meeting, but I remember mine like it was yesterday.

The topic of the meeting was fear and they shared with an honesty I had never heard before. I thought, "What a bunch of candy asses they are to have all those fears." When the chairman called on me I said, "I don't know the meaning of the word fear."

Then the little Nazi they later appointed as my sponsor, because that's the way they did it back then, leaned over and said, "Al, there are a lot of words you don't know the meaning of."

It turns out we were both right. I knew fear alright, only I called it anger. I just didn't know it was fear.

Today I still wonder at some treatment centers saying, "Feelings are not facts." And then telling everyone, "Get in touch with your feelings."

At the end of the meeting someone explained the poker chips. I knew they wanted me to take one. I thought, " No way. I'm a grown man. I'm not going to take one of those tacky little poker chips."

Then another man got up and took one. He looked more like he needed a blood transfusion than a poker chip. But, guess what they did when he went up. They applauded! So, guess what I did. I said, "Well, alright."

As I went up, accompanied by scattered applause, I quickly put together some well chosen words with which to accept my award......They politely declined to listen. And I was now a member of Alcoholics Anonymous.

I had that "peculiar mental twist" Bill W. writes about. I stayed sober for about six weeks. And then one of the members came in from relapsing. They called it a slip. Some of the members told him they hoped he learned something from it. I looked around the room and saw fear on some of their faces, but I'm sure there was none on mine. I thought, "Slips! Wow! Alright! I didn't know we had those!" So I got drunk on the way home from the meeting.

When I got home and walked into the living room my pretty wife was waiting for me with her hands on her hips. She said, "What do you mean coming home drunk? You're not supposed to be drinking, you're a member of Alcoholics Anonymous."

I told her, "I'm not drunk, I'm having a slip. It's part of the program. I'm supposed to learn from it."

Then I put her own stuff back on her, "You work your program, I'll work mine!"

Do you think I had a little problem with honesty?

That began a long period of going in and out of the program. I wanted it, or at least I thought I did, but I just couldn't get it.

I went through a treatment center. The last day I was there, they gave me a homework assignment. They told me to go home, take off all my clothes, stand in front of a full length mirror, hug myself and say, "I love you."

I did that and I have been laughing ever since.

Finally, my wonderful wife could take it no longer and told me she was divorcing me. Now, she had said that before, but I could tell that this time she meant it. In my anger I said, "That's O.K., I can have any woman I please!'

She replied, "That's probably true, you just never have pleased one."

Ouch! That was tough, but as it turns out, the woman's a prophet.

I still haven't pleased one.

I remember that poor woman asking, with tears in her eyes, "Do you have any idea what its like to have you gone for four days and not have any idea where you've been?"

I've wondered a lot lately what would have been the response if I had had the courage and honesty to answer, "Hell, Yes! I know exactly what that feels like!"

"I've been gone for four days and I have no idea where I've been. How do you think that makes me feel? How would you feel if you just discovered that you had been gone for four days and you had no idea where you had been? Pretty scary isn't it?"

No. I never did that and I'm sure no one wanted to listen to that until I walked through the doors of alcoholics Anonymous.

The other members understood and shared with me their similar experiences and the fears, they too, had felt.

What if I could have been proactive instead of reactive?

What if I could have come home drunk to find her waiting up in the living room for me?

What if I could have "headed her off at the pass" by saying everything she was going to say before she had the opportunity to say it?

What if I could have plopped down on the couch with head hung low and said something like, "Well, what do I have to say for myself?"

And then said, "I certainly hope I've learned my lesson this time!"

And then gotten up from the couch and thrown myself out of the house?

And a few minutes and a couple of drinks later gone back and knocked on the door?

And then when she answered the door, said to her, "Well, I knew I'd come crawling back!"

Somehow I suspect none of that would have been appreciated.

I WON'T BE NEEDING

YOUR HELP TODAY.

LOVE

GOD

Chapter 4

I Finally Get It, Zenwise

One day I was finally able to "get it." It was a Zen way of looking at myself and my behavior. I saw not what I was doing, but what I was not doing. Wow! How Zen is that?

The "Big Book" defines alcoholism as a physical allergy combined with a mental obsession. So, if I'm an alcoholic I must be allergic to alcohol.

My allergy to alcohol works exactly like my allergy to poison ivy.

If I come into contact with poison ivy, I'll break out in spots. If I come in contact with a martini, I'll break out in spots like detox, jail and other weird places.

If I come into contact with poison ivy and break out in spots they'll itch. Which will make me want to scratch them. But, if I do it'll spread it and make it itch even more, which will make me want to scratch even more. I'm allergic to poison ivy so scratching makes it itch. I'm not allergic to mosquito bites, when I scratch them they stop itching.

When I drink a martini it makes me want another one more than I wanted the first one. If I have that second martini it'll make me want a third one even more than I wanted either of the first two. I can be knee walking drunk, puking in my shoes and do you know what I want?

That's right, I want another one. That's the allergy. It works just like the poison ivy.

The Chinese have a saying for this phenomenon. They say, "The man takes a drink, then the drink takes a drink (that's the allergy), then the drink takes the man." And that's the last stage of alcoholism.

You see, we're not dealing with simple addiction ere. I'm addicted to cigarettes, but smoking one makes want another one less. I'm addicted to coffee, but when I drink a cup of it, it makes me want another one less.

If you want to increase my desire for cigarettes or coffee you take 'em away. If you want to increase my desire for a drink, you give me one.

Never in my whole life have I ever sat down and drank a six pack of Pepsis. I'm not sure I could.

I know I could not drink a twelve pack of Coca Colas. But, pour about three ounces off the top and fill them back up with rum. Do you think I could drink a twelve pack of those?

Easily! And do know what I would want when I did? That's right another one.

The other half of the disease is mental obsession. I can't prove this but I believe the mental obsession is caused by the allergy. The problem is that mental obsessions are all but invisible to those who have them. I can see yours, and thank God, you can see mine. That's why we need each other. I want you to know that I think yours look ridiculous. What little I can see of my own look very intelligent, rational and reasonable.

So, what I do is substitute some other substance for alcohol and see if a set of behaviors make sense. I like to use broccoli because I know I'm not allergic to it. I know that because when I eat broccoli it makes me want more broccoli less, not more broccoli more.

This is where I see what I was doing by looking at what I would not do. Is that Zen or what?

1...If I were going to a dinner party, I wouldn't eat some broccoli before going there. My wife could never understand why I would drink before going to a cocktail party. Alcoholics will understand.

2...If I were invited to your home for dinner and you served broccoli, I would have some and I'm sure I would enjoy it. But if you didn't I probably wouldn't start to squirm and ask, "Do you have any broccoli in the house?"

3...If someone suggested going to Denny's after a meeting, I probably wouldn't think, "I don't know. Do they serve broccoli there?"

4...And I probably wouldn't go out to the car, reach up under the seat and have a couple of broccolis before we left.

5...And I probably wouldn't have a couple of before dinner broccolis.

6...A couple of broccolis with dinner.

7...An after dinner broccoli or two.

8…A broccoli for the road.

9…And then go home and eat up all the broccoli in the kitchen.

10…And then say to myself, "I think there's some broccoli in the clothes hamper or under the spare tire of the car."

11…And I have never in my whole life ever stood outside of a produce store waiting for it to open!

If I did any of those things, you would have to say I had a serious broccoli problem.

Do you see how ridiculous we are?

Now here's a little test you can take right in the privacy of your own mind. If you understood one word of that, you are a very sick puppy!

Most people who are not alcoholic can make absolutely no sense of that analogy. Once or twice a year my mother would ask me, "Alan, (She always called me Alan) tell me about that broccoli thing again."

So, obviously I was powerless over alcohol. But, was my life unmanageable?

It seems to me that if you do things you don't want to do, your life must be unmanageable whether you're alcoholic or not.

If you have ever been arrested and didn't want to be, your life is unmanageable.

If you have ever ridden in the back seat of a police car, and didn't want to, your life is unmanageable.

Now, if you asked a police officer if you could go for a ride in the back seat his car and he said, "Yes." That's different, but most police officers will say, "No."

If you have ever spent a night in jail and didn't want to, your life is unmanageable.

As a matter of fact, you cannot spend a night in jail just because you want to. If you don't believe me, go up and knock on the door of the jail and tell them you want to spend the night. They won't let you in. You must have an invitation.

If you have ever worn handcuffs and didn't want to, your life is unmanageable. Of course, if it was a sexual thing and you wanted to wear them, that's different.

If you have ever attended a meeting you didn't want to attend, your life is unmanageable.

If you have ever had a probation officer and didn't want one, your life is unmanageable.

If you have ever been to a meeting you didn't want to attend, to get a paper signed that you didn't want to have signed, to take it back to a probation officer you didn't want to have in the first place, your life is totally unmanageable.

If you have ever been thrown out of the house and didn't want to be, your life is unmanageable.

If you have ever lost your spouse and/or children and didn't want to lose them, your life is unmanageable.

If you've ever been evicted and didn't want to be, your life is unmanageable.

If you've ever awakened with a tattoo you can't remember getting, didn't want, and still don't want, your life is unmanageable.

If you've ever had your utilities turned off and you didn't want them turned off, your life is unmanageable.

If you've ever slept in your car when you preferred to sleep in a bed, your life is unmanageable.

If you've ever awakened with someone you didn't want to wake up with, your life is unmanageable.

If you've ever awakened with a total stranger, your life is unmanageable.

If you've ever worn a GPS ankle bracelet and didn't want to wear it, your life is unmanageable.

If you've ever had the tent where you've been living in the woods, blown away in a rain storm, your life is unmanageable.

If you ride a bicycle and don't want to because you no longer have a driver license, your life is unmanageable.

If the bicycle you ride to the convenience store to buy beer is stolen and you can't afford to replace it, your life has become unmanageable

If you've ever gotten a ticket for riding your bike at night without a light while you were on your way to a meeting you didn't want to attend, to get a paper signed that you didn't want to get signed, to take back to a probation officer that you didn't want to have in the first place, all because you couldn't afford to buy a battery for your bicycle light, your life is not only unmanageable, it's a total disaster. (Believe it or not this actually happened. It is not a joke.)

We've heard many times, "Its not how much you drink, but what the drink does to you." When an earth person drinks it's a sedative. If he has two or three drinks and there's nothing going on like a party or a football game, he'll doze off. And, amazingly to me, he develops a desire to stay where he is!

Do you think that's what happens to me? Not hardly! I want to go somewhere. Where do you want to go? I don't care. I'm tired of these people, let's go see those people. Do you have a car? I have a car, lets make a parade out of it. You say you have to go to Chicago? Wait up, I'll go with you."

THE MAN TAKES A DRINK,

THEN THE DRINK TAKES A DRINK,

THEN THE DRINK TAKES THE MAN.

CHINESE PROVERB

Chapter 5

The Zen Way I Came to Belief

My little Nazi sponsor pointed out that in order to believe I could be restored to sanity, I had to understand that I was insane as well as believe that there was a Power greater than myself.

Was I insane? Long before I ever joined AA, I had a spiritual experience somewhat like Bill W's when a brilliant, blinding light came in through the window and a booming voice behind the light said, "Get out of the car and put your hands on the hood!"

It was an angel all dressed in blue.

My history with law enforcement might indicate considerable insanity because I had my own personal police officer. It didn't matter whether I was in Florida, Georgia, Texas or California it was the same cop who pulled me over. I think he was the policeman from the old Dodge commercial with the Smokey hat who would say, "You in a heap o' trouble, boy!"

According to the Highway Patrol at that time I set a speed record on Interstate 95. The speed limit was 70 mph and I was clocked on radar at 15 mph. That's 55mph BELOW the speed limit!

Have you ever noticed how flashing blue lights can bring you out of a blackout? I saw the lights and assumed I was speeding. I looked at the speedometer and pulled over which wasn't hard to do at that speed. My officer walked up to my window which I had somehow managed to put down before he got there. He asked me, "Do you know how fast you were going?"

If I had been honest with him I would have said, "I didn't even know I was in the car!" But, there was one thing I could do drunk just as well as sober. And that was to lie.

I asked him, "Do you hear that noise under the hood?"

He listened and said, "It sounds like a valve to me."

I said, "That's what I thought it was."

I had no idea what a valve was.

He said, "Look, when you want to listen to your engine, pull off the highway. People are going 70 mph past you!"

I thanked him for his advice and he let me go! I could never get away with that today.

I ran into my officer in Ft. Lauderdale. I mean I almost ran INTO him. I had just crossed the city limits on U.S. 1, which they call Federal Highway where the city has beautifully landscaped the safety islands between the north and southbound lanes. At every intersection was a sign that said, "No U Turn." I of course made a U turn and nearly drove right into my officer's police car. He was kind of upset. I told him, "I wanted to go straight but the sign said no, you turn."

He said, "I hope you're leaving town."

I replied, "I certainly am!" And that was the last time he let me go.

Because of my drinking, my life monetarily was chicken one year and feathers the next. During one of those chicken years I was headed north in Merritt Island. I was all suited up and driving a big Cadillac. Itzak Perlman was playing the violin on the stereo I mean Daddy was looking good, and drunk as a hoot owl. I was a one man parade when I came upon a D.U.I. road block.

My officer waved me over and when I lowered my window the aroma of alcohol was strong. Then my officer said, "I've been waiting for you all day." I answered, "I'm sorry, I got here as quick as I could."

He did not let me go.

I used to say, "Let's get drunk and be somebody."

So, things did not always go well with the police when I was busy being somebody. I would become indignant and say things like, "Do you know who I am? I'll have your badge for this. Somebody get his badge number!"

I would wake up the next morning in jail. There would be a card in my pocket with his badge number. Somehow, by that time I had lost all interest in his badge number.

I always knew the U.S. Constitution gave me the right to remain silent, but my ego would not allow me to do that.

One time a police officer asked me for I.D. I told him I didn't have any. He said, "How am I supposed to know who you are?"

It was then that I said the dumbest thing I ever said to a police officer. I replied, "Just keep f**king with me, you'll find out." At that moment another big burly cop came running over and grabbed him for which I will be eternally grateful!

I vaguely remember one time being asked for identification and asking the officer, "Would a silver bullet identify me?"

What do you think? Does any of that indicate the possibility of insanity?

I think it does.

Another example of insanity is the way we deal with our feelings. If you did something to hurt my feelings, I'd get drunk at you. If you hurt my feelings real bad, I'd get drunk and get sick at you. If you hurt my feelings really, really bad, I'd get drunk and get sick and thrown in jail at you and that would fix your ass!

What do you think? Does any of that indicate the possibility of insanity?

I think it does.

Another example of insanity is if we start vast projects with half vast ideas.

I was walking through the mall shortly after Easter, drunk of course, when I passed a pet store. They had bunny rabbits marked way down on sale. I walked in and said, "I want four bunnies, three females and one male. I was going to raise rabbits. Good plan, huh?

By the time I got home with my "livestock", I had become the rabbit baron! I would sell the meat, the fur and the lucky rabbit's feet. Maybe I would franchise this thing and go multinational! My wife is going to be so proud!

I didn't build a cage for the rabbits, I built a rabbit condominium out of two by fours and heavy wire mesh because there were going to be lots and lots of rabbits.

Then I put the male in with one of the females and said, "Go get her, Boy!" But he didn't go get her, if you get my drift. I thought, maybe that female isn't very pretty in rabbit standards although I had picked out for him the one I thought was the prettiest. I was being thoughtful, knowing that that's what I would have wanted if I was in his shoes. So, I put both of the others in with him and he just sat there like he didn't know what to do.

By this time I'm screaming at him, "You call yourself a rabbit? You're a disgrace to the name!" And my poor wife is trying to shut me up because the neighbors can hear all this. I even put him and the pretty one in the living room with the lights turned down low and a little Frank Sinatra on the stereo. Nothing!

Well, we never did get any babies. And we got rid of the rabbits. My kids wouldn't eat chicken for a week because they feared it was rabbit. I guess you can't eat what you have named.

What do you think? Does any of that indicate the possibility of insanity?

I think it does.

My favorite phrase in all of AA literature refers to our "emotional deformities." Holy cow! I'm not just emotional, I'm emotionally deformed! That means I'm an emotional freak! I should be in an emotional side show somewhere.

"Step right up, ladies and gentlemen, and watch this guy freak out, or what ever he does!"

Jim W. says, "Alcoholics are the only people who can be driving down the road absolutely elated and if a traffic light takes too long to turn green, go into the depths of despair."

I was working in Savannah, Georgia when I had one of the most financially successful weeks I had ever had. I was driving my new Camero down Victory Drive. The street was lined with oak trees and stately antebellum mansions. A beautiful symphony was playing on the stereo and I could not have been happier.

Suddenly, I passed a place called The Red Garter. I could see fun seekers going in the door and that pissed me off.

I looked in my Savannah meeting schedule and there were no meetings. Nothing to do but go back to four walls of a crummy motel room. When I got back to my room I looked on the TV schedule saw they had the Playboy channel. Thinking that might cheer me up, I put it on and watched Richard Pryor do fifteen minutes of stand up on the subject of his recovery!

All my life I've heard that God takes care of fools, drunks and working girls. I guess two out of three isn't bad.

I don't know if its true or not, but I'm told that there are only four feelings. And they are mad, sad, glad and scared. In order to have emotions we have to add ego and create them. In other words, feelings are God given and emotions are self inflicted.

Imagine a situation where you are at the bottom of a hill in a narrow alleyway. You look up and see a truck coming down the hill with no one at the wheel. You feel scared. That's a God given feeling and causes an instant injection of adrenaline so you jump out of the way faster than if you had been training for it for months. If the truck passes without hitting you, you feel glad.

Now, that's where well people leave it. They stay glad. They probably think, "Wow, this must be my lucky day. I think I'll buy a lotto ticket."

That's not what most of us alcoholics do. We start thinking and say to ourselves, "Wait a minute. Who's truck is that? Where's the idiot who left it there?"

And then go looking for him. Not being able to find him we get angrier and angrier. And then go to a meeting to bring it up as a topic and work on our anger.

What do you think, does any of that indicate the possibility of insanity?

I think it does.

My little Nazi sponsor suggested that I look around the room at meetings and see the faces of formerly helpless, hopeless drunks who were now happy joyous, and free.

I did and that's how I came to believe. It was really that simple.

He used to tell me to look around the room a lot. One day I was complaining about my lot in life. I wanted to know how I got in the mess that had brought me to Alcoholics Anonymous.

He said, "Look around the room. You may recognize some of us. We were the kids your mother told you not to play with. And do you know what you did? You played with us anyway and that's how you got here."

I said to him one day, "You think you're some kind of Master Sergeant, don't you?"

He reached into his back pocket for his billfold and pulled out a little green and white card with his picture on it. Beneath the picture were the words, United States Air Force Chief Master Sergeant Retired. He said, "Yes, as a matter of fact I do."

I'm not entirely sure I've been restored to sanity. Recently, I was sitting in the back of my boat grooving on the water and the wildlife in God's beautiful world that day.

I saw a mockingbird on the bank repeatedly spreading his wings in a marvelous courtship dance. Above him on the branch of a tree was a female mockingbird. The female was pretending to ignore him, but I could tell she was interested.

I began yelling at him, "Don't do it! Just fly away! I know she's a pretty little thing, but you need to think it through like a drink ! If you go through with what you have in mind I know you'll enjoy it. But, the next thing you know she'll have your ass building a nest!"

"Then you'll wind up sitting on eggs. Later on you'll be flying back and forth, feeding everybody but yourself."

Is that insanity or what?

That mockingbird was doing exactly what God wanted him to do and I was trying to talk him out of it.

To say nothing of the fact that I was talking to a bird!

But I'm not the only one. I have a couple of totally nonsensical things I like to say in a meeting in order to determine who in the group has not been restored to sanity.

The first one is, "I tried day dreaming, but my mind kept wandering."

My favorite one is, "Last night I dreamed I was awake, and when I woke up, I was asleep!"

Any time I have done that in a well attended meeting, I see a few heads nodding in recognition. As if to say, "Yes, I hate it when that happens!"

WHEN I HAVE A HEAD FULL OF ME,

THERE'S NO ROOM IN IT FOR GOD.

COSMIC BILL

Chapter 6

At Last I Let God Take Over

I had decided to move to Tampa and mentioned that to my relatives in Rockledge. They freaked out! "What if we have an emergency?", they cried. "How will we ever get a hold of you?"

I asked my little Nazi what I should do. He said, "Tell them they will have to have the emergency without you."

He asked me, "What if they gave a crisis and you weren't even invited?"

Chapter 4 in the Twelve and Twelve tells us how bad we are at relationships, but every now and then I think I'm ready to inflict myself upon some poor, unsuspecting woman.

I moved to Tampa with a strikingly beautiful woman I met in the program. She had long term sobriety and I just knew it was going to work.

I was wrong.

After only a few days I made a grand exit, telling her to keep everything we had there including money and car and slammed the door on the way out. It was a Hollywood production and worthy, I thought, of an Academy Award. But, I immediately discovered that it was 3 o'clock in the morning, cold and raining. I had with me a small suitcase and a suit on a hanger. I had no money and I knew no one in Tampa to call for help.

I had no more contingency plans, no more "plan B's." I was totally with out of ideas. I had no idea what to do. I was stranded!

Somewhere in the darkness and the rain I went to my knees and turned my will and my life over to the care of God with complete abandon. It was the only choice I had.

Suddenly, I started laughing! All the people who had ever hurt me became funny. Even my situation was funny. Then God reached down and He touched me. He burned me to a crisp. And from those ashes He is building a whole new man.

God is not through building that man, but I already like him a whole lot better than the old one.

Worry has become a thing of the past. Alfred E. Newman has become my patron saint.

Now, I have heard many times in meetings the following analogy;

Three frogs are sitting on a log and one of them decides to jump. How many frogs are still sitting on the log? The answer is three because he only decided to jump. He didn't actually jump.

I may be wrong, but it seems to me like a misunderstanding of what a decision is. Let's suppose there are three drunks sitting on the log and one of them decides to go get a drink.

How many drunks are still on the log? I suspect the answer is probably none. The drunk who decided to go get a drink almost certainly did and the other two probably said, "Sounds like a good idea," and went with him. Now, that's a decision!

I believe the reason it is suggested to make a decision to turn one's will and one's life over to the care of God, is that we have too much house cleaning to do before the decision can actually be carried out.

It seems to me that we are meant to make the decision and keep that decision in mind as we go through the steps until we can actually turn it over like the book says, "with complete abandon."

I also hear a lot about "working the steps." I don't know how to do that. That's not what the book says. It says, "Here are the steps we took." It doesn't say, "Here are the steps we worked."

The trick, if there is one, is to turn it over and not take it back.

My fiend Cosmic Bill talks about having an imaginary gold letter "G" that goes on the front of his sweatshirt. It attaches with Velcro and as long as he can leave it in a drawer, everything is fine.

But occasionally he has a desire to take it out and put it on which means that now Bill is in charge! Things don't go so well until he can take it off and put it back in the drawer.

They are not homework assignments to be "worked" and given to your sponsor to be graded and then move on to the next one. I believe they are steps to be taken and made a part of your life.

I don't believe "It works if you work it." I believe "It works if you live it."

The only place I find the word "work" used in the context of us working is in the promises. One of the promises relates to the loss of the fear of economic insecurity. Obviously, working can be a big help on that one.

Now, I will readily admit that I can talk the talk better than I can walk the walk. But when I leave God's work up to God everything goes so much better. Some say they had to get out of the driver's seat. I had to get out of the whole damn car.

One day, while I was still in Tampa, I spied a deTomaso Pantera, an exotic sports car on a used car lot. Thinking that it might be just the thing for making sales calls, I stopped to look at it. You know, when an alcoholic and a car salesman come together there's some kind of a spiritual connection. The salesman said, "This car is faster than God." Fortunately, I didn't buy the car. But, I was sorely tempted.

But, that salesman was on to something. It has been my experience that when God takes over things happen very quickly. If they move slowly, its usually because I am getting in the way.

So, when I'm not in the way, its like having a tiger by the tail. Sometimes its almost scary. It says somewhere in the scriptures that God's ways are not man's ways. So when God takes over its only natural that I'm not going to under stand what's going on. It seems like chaos. But, when the dust settles and the smoke clears its all fixed. And that's when I want to say, "Oh yeah. That's the way I would have done it.

But its never the way I would have done it.

In fact, some of the things that happen are unpleasant. Some of them are things I would have tried to prevent from happening. But, the final result is always fine and good.

Surprise! Surprise! God knows what He's doing. And I don't.

Its trying to prevent those unpleasant things from happening that sometimes makes me want to get in the way, and that's what slows it down.

So I have two choices. I can turn my will and my life over to the care of God or I can turn my will and my life over to the care of Al. Some choice, huh?

Or as Dr. Phil would say, "How's that working for you?"

I can't prove this, but I believe that the scary part of taking that step is the fear of the loss of control. The loss of what? How can I lose something I never had? I already admitted I didn't have control in the very first step.

I believe we were all like a bunch of ants on a piece of driftwood, floating down the Indian River and every one of them thinking he's steering.

Turning my will and my life over to the care of God has brought an end to worry and fear...even the fear of death.

As a matter of fact I look forward to death. The God of my understanding wants me to do two things; procreate and die. I certainly enjoyed my participation in the first of those and so I expect to enjoy the latter. I think its going to be fun.

I don't know what heaven is like, but I have had some fantasies about it. My favorite is when I die and arrive in heaven there will be a big convention. All of the greatest philosophers, thinkers and orators from throughout all of history will be gathered in a huge auditorium. Winston Churchill will be addressing the throng.

So as not to disturb anyone I slip quietly in and take a seat in the last row. Voltaire and Demosthenes quickly walk to the front and say, "Sit down Winston and be quiet. Al is here."

Now, is that heaven or what?

IT WORKS IF YOU LIVE IT.

BROCCOLI AL

Chapter 7

Where Am I, Anyway

What is it that makes a moral inventory so frightening?

Perhaps its because we almost instinctively know that we are messing around with stuff that usually requires professional help. Maybe, that's why Bill used the word fearless. I think he knew I'd be scared.

It seems to me that the fourth step is brilliantly conceived and poses no risk if the instructions are followed the way they are spelled out in the book. I suggest to you that it is best to do it with the guidance of someone who has already done it himself.

If I am about to take a road trip to somewhere I've never been I need a road map and I also need to know where I'm going. But, none of that is of any help at all unless I can find where I am on that map.

If I am on the path to recovery, I need to know where I am when I start in order to know where I need to go. Else how am I going to get there? But, somewhere inside of me I really didn't want to know where I was.

My little Nazi told me to quit procrastinating and get on with it. I don't like to think of it as procrastination. I prefer to think of it as "creative foot dragging." There is also something inside of me that really doesn't like doing anything that's good for me. I also loved doing anything that isn't. I remember watching my parents having a cup of coffee with breakfast.

So I asked, "May I have a cup of coffee?"

They said, "No. Its not good for you."

Wow, I really wanted one then! It was a big people drink and when I was finally allowed to have one, it tasted terrible. I had to add milk and sugar to cover up the taste and I loved it. I still do.

I didn't want to take any of the steps. And yet I actually enjoyed taking them. And I felt so much better when I did. And I would say to my little Nazi, "That was great, let's do it again!"

He would always say, "No, let's go on to the next one."

"I don't want to."

WHO HAS DECEIVED THEE

AS OFTEN AS THYSELF?

BEN FRANKLIN

Chapter 8

Why Should I Tell You

I certainly did not want to admit my wrongs to God or anybody else. I recall a story of a preacher being asked to pray for a practicing alcoholic. He looked skyward and prayed, "Lord, please help this poor old drunk."

And the drunk cried, "Don't tell Him I've been drinking."

I know that doesn't make sense. It also didn't make sense to me that I needed to admit my wrongs to myself because I already knew what they were.

It didn't make sense to admit them to God because He already knew what they were, too.

And what did another human being need with that information?

It didn't make sense then and it still doesn't. I just know that those who don't do it, don't stay sober. It doesn't have to make sense and here's how I know that.

I met and married my second wife in the fellowship.

I was sitting in a meeting one day and I looked across the

room at a pretty redhead. Right then I decided I wanted what she had and I was willing to go to any lengths to get it.

She said, "Then you're ready to take certain steps."

At some of them I balked. I thought I could find an easier softer way, but I could not. And so we were married in an AA club house right after a meeting during the holidays. We even had Santa Claus in attendance.

I should have read "How it Works" because that's exactly how it worked, right on down to, "we tried to hold on to our old ideas" and the result was nil. So, she rightly let go of me completely. That was my second divorce.

She will always have a special place in my heart because she left me with a very Zen idea that I have shared in many meetings (always giving her the credit).

It is an idea that has spared me a great deal of pain and brought me a lot of happiness.

I can't recall what we were arguing about. But, she said something that made no sense at all to me. And when I said, "Jane, that doesn't make any sense," she said, "It doesn't have to."

CHECKMATE! She was right! She had won the argument with one masterful stroke!

I have applied that thought to almost every aspect of my life.

Almost nothing has to make sense. I always thought it did. I don't know why I thought that, I just did.

Many things in this world don't make sense. And I used to

have to try to make sense out of them. I don't have to do that any more. What a relief!

Whenever I encounter a situation that doesn't make sense, I remind myself to remember that Jane said, "It doesn't have to."

So, today two of my heroes are Jane and Walter Cronkite who used to end every newscast with the words, "And that's the way it is."

"There's two theories about arguing with a woman. Neither one of them works!"..... Will Rogers

Those who do not take the inventory and admit their wrongs are almost sure to drink.

THAT DOESN'T MAKE SENSE!

IT DOESN'T HAVE TO.

JANE B.

Chapter 9

Slippers Monotonous

If you have never had a slip, you have missed a lot. You haven't missed anything good, but you have missed something. There isn't much in this world worse than a head full of AA and a belly full of booze!

I'm a great fan of AA bumper stickers, especially for new comers. If you decide to drink, you have to take the stickers off of your car which gives you time to think it through. Because you can't park your car in a gin mill parking lot with those stickers hanging all over it.

And you haven't lived until you go to pay your bar tab and have your white chip roll out across the floor. That's when you find out who the alcoholics are because they pretend not to see it. They look away. If there is a civilian in the place he'll say, "You dropped a poker chip." He doesn't think anything of it.

Then you get up off the barstool, walk to the door and open it just a crack. You look up and down the street to see if anybody from AA is out there because they have spies. You don't want to get busted by the AA police.

I told a bartender, "Just put the bottle up on the bar." He did and it was a bottle of Ancient Age, great big red letters A. A. I didn't know we had our own whiskey!

And the mirror behind the bar goes from being a really good friend to being an enemy. I used to look in the mirror, fix my tie, smile and hold my cigarette just right. I mean Daddy would be looking good! But once I really understood what an insane thing I was doing, the mirror made me watch myself doing it.

I have said some really dumb things to police officers, but I think the dumbest thing I ever said to anybody was to a bartender. He poured me a short shot and I complained by saying, "Hey! Half measures avail us nothing."

And I can tell you if you drink long enough and stay alive long enough this will happen to you. You will be sitting on a barstool, half in the bag with a drink in your hand. There will be a decent man or woman sitting on the barstool next to you. He or she will turn to you with a drink in his or her hand and say to you, "This stuff is killing me, but I can't stop drinking it. What do you think I should do?"

What are you going to say? What are you going to do? I'll tell you what you're going to do. You are going to twelve step that person and then hope to God he or she turns around and twelve steps you.

What else can you do? This person is a brother or a sister.

What a terrible tragedy it is when people in AA go back to drinking.

Without recovery it ends with one of the three B's……the Bug House, the Big House or the Bone Yard.

My little Nazi sponsor was a master of understatement. He used to say, "Alcoholics who drink do not do well."

And speaking of understatement, he was the first person to tell me to "get off the pity pot."

I remember thinking, "Pity pot! How dare you call what I'm going through a pity pot? I've never heard of pity pots before, but they must have little flowers, birds and bunny rabbits painted on them. I'm not on a pity pot I'm all the way down to the bottom of the sewer."

ALCOHOLICS WHO DRINK

DO NOT DO WELL

AL'S LITTLE NAZI

Chapter 10

Take This Away From Me

I don't know if I have ever been entirely ready to have every one of my character defects removed. I probably love some of them.

Isn't that silly. I may enjoy them, but they aren't making me happy. In fact, my character defects are what got me into the mess that required my joining AA in the first place. So, something must be done about them. Just going to meetings isn't going to do it. "Sitting in a garage will not make me turn into a car."…….Cory S.

If I'm not entirely ready to have a character defect removed, then obviously its not going to do any good to work on it. Apparently it doesn't do an alcoholic much good to work on it anyway. It doesn't do any harm to work on it, it just doesn't do much good. For years I read every self improvement book that came down the pike. I even did what some of them said and I never improved.

I hear many say, "The only thing I can change is me." I believe just the opposite. I believe the only thing I can't change is me. I must rely upon God for that and I give Him the credit for any and all positive changes in me that have taken place.

They have a saying in Georgia that I dearly love, and it goes like this:

"Don't try to teach a pig to sing. You'll waste your time and really annoy the pig."

How do I know when I'm entirely ready to have a character defect removed? When it has caused me so much pain that I'm desperate to have it removed. Then I'm probably ready.

If you have reached this stage in your program you should know it works. By now you have had the compulsion to drink removed. Almost any civilian will tell you that excessive drinking is by itself a major character defect. And for a Being who can remove an alcoholic's compulsion to drink, parting the Red Sea must be like child's play.

So, how do we go about the removal of a character defect or shortcoming?

If we are entirely ready, we humbly ask God to remove it. Isn't that beautiful in its simplicity?

If you are a thief, you humbly ask God to remove the desire to steal and in the meantime don't steal anything. So, what do you do in the meantime? Well, it's just a mean time.

Isn't that the way your compulsion to drink was removed? That's the way mine was.

Sometimes a character defect is removed instantly. God certainly has that ability. I have had my resentments removed in just that manner.

I was going through a divorce I didn't want. I was staying in the house which was sold but not yet closed.

There was no furniture remaining in it except for a mattress upon which I slept. I was lonely and wallowing in self pity. And it was Father's Day.

Every hour or so I would go to the mailbox to see if there was a Father's Day card. See how silly and pathetic I was because Father's Day is on Sunday and there is no mail delivery on Sunday. But, I continued to check the mail all day.

I had been invited to dinner at the home of a lady I didn't like. I accepted the invitation because I knew I needed to get out of the house. I dawdled over dinner to put off going home, so it was late when I got there.

I checked the mail one more time and went to bed without even turning on the lights.

As I lay there in the darkness my resentments began to build up. I could think of nothing else. It was as if they began to surround me and speed up. They were spinning faster and faster. They were out of control and so was I! I was frightened. I feared I was about to have a psychotic episode. I had never had one but I had heard of them.

Suddenly, out of nowhere, came a thought, "Were entirely ready...."

Immediately, everything stopped and I was calm. I got down on my knees and I prayed, "God I'm helpless. Please take these resentments away from me, I can't handle it anymore."

Immediately I felt a peace come over me and I saw in the mind's eye an ocean upon which floated little vignettes of all the major events in my life. There were wins and losses, triumphs and disasters and they all looked the same. One was no more important than the other.

There was a wonderful sense of peace. I could have gone right to sleep. But I stayed awake as long as I could, just grooving on the feeling.

The next morning when I got up, I went out into the living room and there on the floor were two Father's Day cards. Both of my kids had visited me while I was at that lady's house and had brought the cards with them.

Oddly enough, yesterday was also Father's day and this time no one called or sent a card and it was OK.

If you look around the room of any meeting you will see the faces of people with whom you can, and often do trust your life. But, because not all of us have had all of our character defects removed, there are those with whom you may not be able to trust your money. That's why, at the end of a meeting, its traditional to hold hands when we close our eyes to pray.

There is an old story of Saint Peter taking a newcomer on a tour of heaven. He explains that many things that were sins on earth are not sins in heaven and vise versa. He also says that everything in heaven is perfect. But, what would be perfect for one person would not be for another, so there are different areas for different people.

They went into one area where there was a huge bar-b-que picnic with people gorging themselves. Saint Peter said, "These people are Jews who were not allowed pork back on Earth. They're making up for that now."

Upon entering another area there was a big dance party with everybody dancing. No one was sitting out even one dance. He said, "These people are Southern Baptists who were not allowed to dance back on Earth. They're making up for that now."

The next area was really depressing. People were sitting around in rocking chairs, watching the weather channel, bored out of there minds. "These people are alcoholics. They've already done everything!"

SITTING IN A GARAGE

WILL NOT

MAKE ME TURN INTO A CAR

CORY S.

Chapter 11

Loaves and Fishes

There is a Zen story of two holy men or monks who were travelling on foot because that's the way they travel. They came upon a beautiful princess who was trying to cross a stream. The stream had become swollen to overflowing from recent rains. They could tell she was royalty by her clothing.

The older of the two monks picked her up, waded the across the stream and deposited her on the other side. He then continued on his way.

Monks don't talk much, and they traveled for several hours without speaking. Finally the other monk said, "We're not supposed to even talk to women, much less pick one up and carry her."

To which the first monk replied, "I left her back by the stream. Why are you still carrying her?"

In order to avoid the torture of carrying with me the wrongs of my past it was necessary to list all those I had wronged and become willing to make amends to them all. That was the beginning of freedom from the past. I needed to make the list as best as I could remember. Making the list was fairly easy. But then I had to be willing to make the amends, that was the hard part.

There were many who had harmed me as much as I had harmed them. Some had harmed me even more. Why should I make amends to them? There's no justice in that.

We're not looking for justice. We're looking for freedom. We desire freedom from the guilt of the kind of alcoholics we used to be. We desire the freedom to walk with our heads held high, unafraid of meeting up with someone to whom we owe money or other restitution.

I can remember walking into a store where I had never been. The store owner said, "You have a lot of nerve coming in here again!"

There was someone who looked just like me who would go out at night and create all manner of havoc. The next day I would have to go out and repair the damage that idiot had done. It was a real Jeckel and Hyde situation.

It didn't matter what the others had done. It only mattered what I had done.

At the first level we do it because it is therapeutic.

At a higher level we do it because it makes us free.

At the highest level we do it because it is the right thing to do.

When I looked at the financial amends to be made it was obvious to me that it would probably be impossible to complete the task in my lifetime. But, somehow it turned out to be something like the loaves and fishes.

Some of those I owed had disappeared and could not be found. A few even pointed out that I owed them less than I thought. Some even refused my offer of amends saying, "Just don't drink and don't rip anybody else off."

I think some of those who refused would rather hate me than get their money back. A few years ago I spoke at a gratitude dinner. There was dance following the talk when a very attractive lady came up to me and angrily reminded me that I owed her sixty dollars and had for a long time. I had completely forgotten about it, but she was right. I didn't have sixty dollars on me at the time so I asked for her address and said I'd mail it to her. She refused and stormed off in a huff.

Another type of amends comes from lying, particularly about another person. It might be helpful to have already stopped lying as a character defect back in steps six and seven. If I have told a lie about someone to another person or persons which could damage his or her reputation, then I must go to that person and confess what I have done so the person knows what happened to him and can deal with it. But first, I need to go to every person I told the lie to so they will know it was not the truth.

Oddly enough, this sort of thing seems to happen more in sobriety than it did when we were still drinking. It flies around the rooms like wildfire, only we call it gossip. I have had to accept the fact that women gossip. Men, on the other hand, analyze and discuss rumors which is a lot more scientific.

I apologize for that last paragraph. It doesn't mean a thing. I just love saying it.

WE'RE NOT LOOKING

FOR JUSTICE,

WE'RE LOOKING

FOR FREEDOM.

BROCCOLI AL

Chapter 12

I Claim the Right To Be Wrong

I wish I could say I do my daily inventory every day. I wish I could but I can't. I just plain forget to do it. That's the one area of my life that I simply don't walk the walk anywhere near as well as I talk the talk. Life goes much better when I do it, but sometimes I get busy and forget. Maybe that's a character defect that needs to be removed.

One of my favorite things I have learned to do is to admit when I'm wrong. Sometimes I'm wrong and don't know it. But, when I do know it and admit it promptly its wonderful.

I have no idea why it used to be so important to be right. Maybe that was one of the old ideas I had to let go of. I can remember when I would make a decision that turned out to be wrong, I would run around like a chicken with its head cut off changing everything else in order to make it turn out right.

I can remember overhearing two total strangers in conversation in the street and one of them saying something I thought was wrong. And I would feel a desire to stop and straighten him out.

I'm told there's a tomb stone in Key West that says, "I told you I was sick." I guess it was important to that guy to be right, too. I can relate to that.

Back when I was still angry all the time, I would've wanted one that said, "Hey! What are you looking at?"

Sometimes I admit I'm wrong so quickly it angers people because they don't believe its sincere. Their skepticism is understandable because I abuse this principle by admitting I'm wrong when I don't even think I am. That's how unimportant being right is to me today.

"You were wrong!"

"Yes, I was wrong."

"Well, you were wrong in being wrong."

"Yes, I was wrong about that, too."

Isn't that beautiful? Isn't that freeing? And nothing could be more non-confrontational. Its not easy to pick a fight with me.

**MAKE AMENDS QUICKLY,
CROW IS EASIER TO EAT
WHEN IT'S FRESH.**

BROCCOLI AL

Chapter 13

Meditation — The Way To God

I hear people saying, "This program is simple, but its hard." I don't believe that. I believe we make it hard. I know I did.

Looking back on it, the program was easy. But, it was hard for me because I found a hard way to do it almost the whole way. So, it's a good thing it was easy.

I could not have done it if it was hard because if you do something that's hard the hard way, it's almost impossible. But if you do something that's easy the hard way, you at least have a shot. I have watched many, many others do the same thing. I'm surprised we don't all make love standing up in a hammock.

I asked my little Nazi, "How do you meditate?"

He asked me, "Do you really want to know?"

"Yes."

"OK. Shut up and listen."

So I shut up and listened. He didn't say anything. So, I said, "Well?"

"Well what?"

"HOW DO YOU MEDITATE??"

He looked at me like I was really stupid and said, "Shut up and listen. That's how you do it, preferably at a time and place where its quiet and peaceful, without distraction."

See what I mean? Its simple and easy as long as I don't try to complicate everything.

That was the day I learned how to increase my conscious contact with God. Prior to that I had tried music, weird postures and even meditation tapes. All of those things were merely distractions.

Keep it simple, stupid.

A potential Zen neophyte had traveled on foot for many days to arrive at the door of a famous Zen temple. Upon being admitted he was given a bowl of rice gruel to eat. He then asked permission for an audience with the Temple Master. He asked the Temple Master, "Tell me what to do."

The Temple Master asked, "Have you eaten your rice gruel?"

"Yes, I have."

"Then wash your bowl."

Keep it simple, stupid.

I have found meditation to be enormously beneficial to me. Without it I can lose my Step Three.

That's the reason I don't like making early morning appointments. Because whenever I do, I invariably over sleep.

When that happens, I fly out of bed, spray on a little "no-bath", don yesterday's clothes, run out the door, jump in the car and Al's in charge. I can assure you, that day is a disaster until I can stop and start the day over.

SHUT UP AND LISTEN

AL'S LITTLE NAZI

Chapter 14

We Awaken and Pay the Bill

I'm told that when a scribe was interviewing Buddha, he asked, "Are you a god?"

Buddha replied, "No."

Then he asked, "Are you a messiah?"

"No."

"Are you a prophet?"

"No."

"Then what are you?"

And he replied, "I am awake."

Like most of us my spiritual awakening was of the educational variety. It took place over a period of time as I went through the steps.

Trying to define or describe it to someone who has not experienced it is, to me, almost an exercise in futility.

I've been asked by newcomers, "How will I know when I've had a spiritual awakening?"

I can only reply, "You'll know."

I've been asked, "What's it like."

The only way I know to explain it is its like going from black and white to Technicolor. The whole world looks different.

I had been in the program for a very few weeks when my little Nazi called me and said, "Get dressed and ready to go. We're going on a twelve step call."

"I don't know what to say!"

"You're not going to say anything. You have nothing to say."

The man we went to see was a local golf pro and golf equipment shop owner. He was shaking pretty badly.

He listened politely but unimpressed. And my little Nazi was laying some really good stuff on him. He wanted to know how long my sponsor had been sober, which was three and a half years. Still unimpressed, he turned to me with the same question.

I told him, "Almost six weeks."

He was impressed with that and said, "Wow!"

Somehow there seems to be fewer "formal" twelve step calls today then there were when I first joined AA. And that's sad because it gave us a chance to see first hand the damage that we ourselves had caused. Its easier to see it in others than it is in ourselves. Its also an area of life you don't get to see in meetings.

You see spouses almost take offence at the alcoholic's sobriety. Its somewhat understandable if you think of the relationship's history. Here's a woman who has done everything she could think of to sober him up. She has had the preacher over, pored his whiskey down the sink, withheld sex, threatened to leave and take the kids, and followed him to the bars to stop him.

Then one day two guys from AA show up. One is an unemployed carpenter and the other is a bricklayer who can't lay brick straight. Her husband rides off with them and never drinks again. Wouldn't that piss you off?

Sometimes, you go on a call with an AA buddy and knock on the door. A very frightened woman answers the door. She doesn't know if you are police, process servers, bill collectors or what. So, someone's anonymity has to be broken and you say something like, "We're from AA and George has expressed an interest in doing something about his drinking."

Then you see an instant personality change. "Come in! Can I get you a cup of coffee, a piece of pie, or anything?"

So, you share your experience, strength and hope with George and if he's in good enough shape you offer to take him to a meeting. If he responds and wants to go to a meeting, you see another instant personality change.

"He can't be seen going to meetings, he'll lose his job."

"But, Lady, he's dying."

"That's OK, he's insured."

The relationship has deteriorated to that point.

I believe the first eleven steps allow God to give us our sobriety and the twelfth step is where we pay the bill. And if we don't pay it we may have our sobriety repossessed.

"If you want happiness for an hour...take a nap If you want happiness for a day.... go fishing If you want happiness for a month. get married If you want happiness for a year...inherit a fortune If you want happiness for a lifetime help someone." Chinese Proverb

I would like to share with you one of my earliest spiritual awakenings.

It has to do with cliches. There are many cliches in Alcoholics Anonymous, not just the ones on the wall in the meeting rooms. They include things like:

"Meeting Makers Make It."

"Keep Coming Back."

"Take the cotton out of your ears and put it in your mouth"

"Don't quit before the miracle happens."

And of course, many, many others.

One dreary, rainy Sunday night in a meeting held upstairs over a place called Shorty's Bar, I heard a whole set of cliches I had never heard before and have not heard since.

There were only six or seven people in attendance including an old man who was passing through on his way to Miami.

He claimed to have thirty years of sobriety and this was back when almost nobody had that much time. He also claimed that he was the first person to ever be arrested for public drunk in the city of Milwaukee.

I say "claimed" because I don't know. But, I would place my bets that every word this very spiritual man spoke was the truth.

He spoke many cliches, many of which have been lost to me in the murkiness of time. He didn't call them cliches, but you could easily tell that they were.

He said the old timers in Milwaukee never argued with or tried to scare a new comer.

They didn't try to scare a newcomer with talks about the yets. The newcomer would say, "I never got a DUI, I never got fired, I never got divorced, etc, etc, etc."

The old timers would then reply with, "Great! If you don't drink, go to meetings and do what we tell you, you'll get to keep all your nevers."

If the new comer said, "I don't know if I am an alcoholic or not."

Our man would reply, "We don't know if you're an alcoholic or not either. If you're NOT an alcoholic, and you don't drink, go to meetings and do what we tell you, you'll never become one."

"If, you ARE an alcoholic, and you don't drink, go to meetings and do what we tell you, you won't get any sicker than you are right now."

"I don't even know if I'm an alcoholic. But, when I drink, I drink like one and I drink just like you do."

He told us that he moved from Milwaukee to Baltimore where there were only five sober alcoholics in the whole city.

While he was there the membership grew to over fifty in only a couple years.

And then, sudden tragedy. In one weekend more than half of them got drunk.

The old gentleman said that he had observed only one member, drunk or sober, who was happy. He said, "I couldn't understand why he was happy. I knew his wife and we called her bullet lips. But, I wanted what he had and I was willing to go to any lengths to get it."

He asked the man to sponsor him and it turns out that what the man had was the new "Big Book." It was the only one in Baltimore.

He said, "I started through the steps and I was doing great until I came to Step Two. I had great difficulty with that and so being a good alcoholic, I wanted to get my information from the horses mouth."

"So I got in my car and I drove to New York to see Bill I told him that I was an engineer and a scientist and that I knew nothing about things spiritual."

He told us he asked Bill, "Tell me about your Higher Power."

Bill said, "That's not the program. You need your own conception of a Higher Power."

He told Bill, "I understand that, but I don't know where to start. Maybe if you'll tell me about yours, I can build one from there."

And Bill replied, "OK mine chooses to remain anonymous, so I call him Jesus C."

I AM AWAKE

BUDDHA

Chapter 15

'Tis the Season to Be Sorry

"ALTHOUGH NO ONE CAN GO BACK AND MAKE A NEW BEGINNING, ANYONE CAN START FROM NOW AND MAKE A NEW ENDING."

UNKNOWN

Along about the middle of October many alcoholics, especially newcomers, begin psyching up to be depressed for the holidays. And most of the meeting halls in our area begin scheduling "depress-a-thons" where the rooms will be open for twenty four or more hours. I remember a dance being cancelled in Tampa in order to hold a "depress-a-thon."

Many of us begin worrying about how we're going to stay sober during Thanksgiving, Christmas, and New Years Eve. For many of us those holidays have been disasters in the past. Also, they have never lived up to their advance billing. There is a "Christmas Card" commercial for one the breweries that shows a horse drawn sleigh pulling up to a big house where everyone inside is singing carols. I don't know about you, but I've never even seen horse drawn sleighs except as road signs for antique shops in New England.

I know today that I cannot stay sober this coming Christmas. As I write these words it is May 16. I can only stay sober May 16 on May 16.

Wow, how Zen is that? Zen is about now and now is where I like to live.

Another thing causing problems for many of us during the holidays comes in the form of invitations. "I have to go to the company Christmas party. I have to attend the wedding. I have to go to the family reunion. I have to....., I have to....., I have to.......

Almost any time an alcoholic begins a sentence with the words, "I have to" he is telling himself a lie.

Alcoholics are people who have to do anything they don't know they don't have to do. So, if they don't know they don't have to do it, then they have to do it. But, once they know they don't have to do it then they don't have to do it any more.

Here's a little test you can take in the privacy of your own mind. If you understood one word of the above paragraph, you are one sick puppy!

But it seems to be true in every aspect of my life, including my drinking. I had to drink because I didn't know I didn't have to drink. Since I didn't know I didn't have to drink, I had to drink. But, once I truly understood that I didn't have to drink, then I didn't have to drink anymore.

I didn't have to go to a party simply because I was invited. I didn't have to go to the office Christmas party and the truth is probably no one would even know that I wasn't there or for that matter even care.

If I don't go to the wedding, the bride and groom will be just as married.

If I don't go to the family reunion, most people there will be glad.

One of my favorite stories about the holidays involves two psychiatrists who meet in the hallway of a psychiatric hospital. One of them asks, "How was your Thanksgiving?"

The other one says, "Terrible, we had dinner at my mother's and I made a Freudian slip at the table."

"Oh, no! What did you say?"

"Well I meant to say Mom, please pass the potatoes, but instead I said You ruined my life, you f**king bitch!"

The holidays are not the only time it is necessary to turn down a drink.

I am fond of fine dining. When the cocktail waitress asks if I want a before dinner drink or the sommelier suggests a bottle of wine I usually say, "No thanks. I've had enough already."

God knows I'm telling the truth. But, they assume I've already been drinking. When I do that they always back off immediately. They don't want their furniture broken up.

Most folks don't know or care what we are drinking. I certainly didn't know or care what they were drinking as long as they weren't drinking mine. My first wife usually tried to control my drinking by saying, "No thanks. I'll just have some of his."

"Like hell you will."

In turning down a drink, I've always wanted to say something like, "No thanks. I have to be in Muskogee in October."

It is extremely rare for anyone to question you about not drinking but it can happen. Usually, it is a sufficient explanation to say, "I'm not drinking tonight."

John, a friend of mine in recovery had a dinner date with woman he understood to not be an alcoholic. She ordered a cocktail and he ordered a cup of coffee. She questioned him about it and would not leave it alone, even after he told her he was an alcoholic. She kept telling him that one drink wouldn't hurt him.

Finally, John said, "Apparently, you don't know what its like to wake up in the wee hours of the morning in the ditch of a desolate country road without a house or car in sight, beaten, battered and bleeding from every orifice."

She was horrified and asked, "Is that what happens to you when you drink?"

"No," he said, "That's what might happen to YOU if I drink."

He tells me she never went out with him again.

LAUGHING CAN ADD EIGHT YEARS TO YOUR LIFE.

AIG TV COMERCIAL

Chapter 16

Three Kinds of Weird Alcoholics

Having fun is serious business. Sobriety is not enough. Sobriety is a tool for being happy and having fun is part of happiness.

I had seen the help wanted ads in the newspaper. All the crummy jobs said, "Must be sober and reliable." The president of the company didn't have to be either sober or reliable. But, somebody had to be trusted with the key to the building, to open on time in the morning and lock it up at closing time. That person was generally the janitor or custodian.

So, when I went to my first meeting I feared that all the fun and excitement of life was over. I feared that we would all just sit around and be SOOOBURRRR. How positively dreadful!

I soon found, much to my dismay, that there were those who seemed to do just exactly that. Praise the Lord they were a small minority. But, they were a loud minority.

There were three kinds of alcoholics I could neither understand nor relate to. The three types I didn't and still don't understand, I call the "Aware People", the "Long Timers" and the "Grinders."

"The Aware People"

The Aware People would say things like, "Well, I still have all the problems I ever had, but today I'm aware of them." Then they would smile, pleased and grateful for the progress they had made.

What progress? It didn't sound like a great deal of growth to me. That's akin to saying, "Well, I don't have a job and I haven't had one for a year and a half, but today I'm aware that I don't have a job."

"The Long Timers"

The Long Timers would say things like, "Well, I didn't get in the shape that brought me here overnight and its going to take a long, long, long time for me to get any better at all."

I would look at them and think, "Buddy, you can count on that."

"The Grinders"

Now, if I'm about to make fun of your sponsor and that pisses you off, well..... that's OK, it'll give you something to stay home and work on.

I say that because grinders tend to sponsor a lot of people.

The Grinders say things like, "I'm sober, Gawd Dammit. I've worked those steps and I've trudged that road. No pain, no gain." And then they say, "If you want what I have and you're ready to go to any lengths to get it……"

I thought then and I think now, "I don't want anything you have."

Incidentally, if you look up the word trudge in a 1930's dictionary you'll find that the number one definition is "slow careful steps." It doesn't mean slogging through mud up to your neck.

Grinders tend to speak with carefully cultivated whiskey voices. They also tend to be not much better off financially then they were when they first arrived at the program.

They often give the impression that poverty is the price of sobriety. If you decide to go back to school, start a business, buy a house or try for a promotion they will tell you, "You better watch out! You're going to get drunk.!"

I don't know why these poor souls are the way they are. Maybe its alcoholic brain damage. I don't like brain damage, my brain is my second favorite organ.

The worst of the Grinders are what I call AA Bullies. The big book is an instrument of recovery but they seem to think its a weapon with which to beat up newcomers.

Maybe they are that way because not drinking is the only success they have ever had. Some of them have been dry for so long they're fire hazards.

Many, if not most of the grinders can quote chapter and verse from the Big Book and yet fail to grasp the joy in it.

In fact many of the grinders are considered to be Gurus.

I have often thought that we ought to have Guru meetings where the only requirement for attendance is that you must be a Guru. It really would not be difficult to qualify because Gurus are self appointed.

During the meeting there would be no topic. Instead,

they would go around the room and each Guru would give five minutes of his or her best stuff. And then everyone in attendance would laugh and then tell him to keep coming back.

"THE PURPOSE OF A FISH TRAP IS TO CATCH

FISH, AND WHEN THE FISH ARE CAUGHT,

THE TRAP IS FORGOTTEN.

THE PURPOSE OF A RABBIT SNARE IS TO CATCH

RABBITS, AND WHEN THE RABBITS ARE CAUGHT,

THE SNARE IS FORGOTTEN.

THE PURPOSE OF WORDS IS TO CONVEY IDEAS.

WHEN THE IDEAS ARE GRASPED, THE WORDS

ARE FORGOTTEN.

WHERE CAN I FIND A MAN WHO HAS FORGOTTEN

WORDS? HE IS THE ONE I WOULD LIKE TO TALK TO"

CHUANG—TZU

Chapter 17

Fun, Fun, Fun

Having fun is serious business. And most of us have no idea how to have it. I knew how to get drunk and chase women. But, if drinking is fun, I've had about all the fun I can stand, thank you.

As a matter of fact, drinking is boring. If you don't think so, get a quart of soda, juice, tea or something that has no alcohol in it. And drink the whole quart with a shot glass. Not that I ever had much use for shot glasses.

When I got sober, one of the things I didn't know was how to play. I knew how to play games that had rules. I knew that in a softball game, if I got a hit, I didn't run to third base. I knew how to play poker and other card games. But, plain unstructured play was something I knew nothing about.

I watched children to see how they did it. The kid would knock on the door. And when the Mommy answered the door, the kid would ask, "Can Johnny come out and play?" And if the Mommy said yes, Johnny would go out and play.

If the kid had said, "Can Al come out and play?"

I would have had to say, "I don't know. What are you playing? Because, I don't know if I know how to play that."

It was suggested that I mentally go back to my childhood and look for things I wanted to do then, but wasn't able to because I wasn't big enough. I knew that I no longer wanted to be a cowboy or a policeman or even a fireman.(Although, I would like to ride the fire truck one time and ring the bell.)

I did want to be an airplane pilot ever since I was a little boy. So I went to a little one runway airport which had half a dozen small airplanes. It was next to a drive-in theater that showed dirty movies. The airport had a dilapidated sign at its entrance saying, "Flying Lessons."

There was an old trailer with a sign saying, "Office."

I told the gentleman inside that I wanted to make an appointment for a flying lesson. He said, "Why make an appointment? Why not go now?"

"You don't give me any time to psych up."

"I don't give you time to chicken out either."

Not only was this something I couldn't do as a little boy it was something I was pretty sure they wouldn't let me do drunk, either.

As we walked over to the little Cessna 150 airplane, he asked me how much I weighed. When I told him, he added my weight to his and said, "Well, we can't quite fill the tanks."

He almost lost his student right then.

After walking around the plane and checking out wing flaps, rudders etc. we took off and flew to 1500 feet. At that point my instructor took his hands off the controls and said, "Its your airplane."

I said, "I don't know what these things do."

And he said, "Move them around. You'll find out."

I was to get a valuable lesson in program as well as in flying. Because when you get the airplane all cockeyed and don't know what to do, you take your hands off the controls and the plane straightens itself out and flies straight. Just like life! Let go and let God.

I only took the lessons long enough to do one solo. The Federal Aviation Administration had made it clear that I was not ever going to get a pilot's license because of my past DUIs.

I believe we all need to find new ways to play and have fun. Probably the only way to do that is to try as many different things as possible. Some of them you will like and some of them you won't like. If you try something and you don't like it, so what? Go on to something else.

Some folks think I went a little far when I went parachuting. But, you might want to try it. I promise you that even if you don't like it, you won't be bored.

I came across an ad in the Yellow Pages for a parachute school. I called them and got a price for ground school, instructor, airplane and two jumps. (Static Line Descents they called them.)

It would cost less than a typical night of bar hopping. I used to spill more than that. But, I asked, "Why two jumps? I only wanted to go once so I could say I had done it."

I was told, "We always schedule two because you'll be so busy freaking out on the first one, you won't have time to groove on the experience."

I called two friends in recovery and they both agreed to go with me.

So, one Saturday we spent almost the whole day jumping off of a four foot high platform and climbing in and out of the airplane, practicing how to do it. Then late in the afternoon we climbed into the aircraft and took off.

Aboard were the pilot, the instructor and three terrified "heroes."

We flew to 3000 feet and the instructor opened the door. At his direction the other two guys went first. Then it was my turn.

With great difficulty I sat on the floor and dangled my feet out the door. (That's funny, it wasn't all that hard to do that when the plane was on the ground.) Then, as I was taught, I climbed out the wing strut and stood with one foot on the airplane's tire.

At that time the instructor yelled to me that it had taken me too long to get out there which caused us to over fly our drop zone. He said, "Stay where you are, we're going to make a go around!"

I yelled, "Do you know where I am? I'm half way out the wing of an airplane!" I was also up to page 34 in the hymnal. I felt like I was starring in some kind of Laurel and Hardy movie.

I did what he said. And when I jumped, instead of looking at a sunset, I was in one! What a wonderful, exciting and spiritual way to end the day!

OK! I went a little overboard. But, you get the idea.

Unstructured play, when mixed with insanity can be bizarre and lots of fun. A couple of friends and I went to an all night coffee shop after a late night meeting for pie and coffee.

There was a large glass case on the wall with quite an assortment of pies. We each had a piece of pie and it was really good, so seconds seemed to be in order.

When the waitress came for our order, I asked her, "How much pie do you have? I might want to buy all of it."

After much convincing she counted up the pies counting the unsliced ones as six. She presented me with a bill and I bought all the pie in the restaurant. We left the pies in the case for now.

Presently, a nice looking man sat down at a table and ordered a piece of pie. And I heard the waitress tell him, "I'm sorry sir, we're all out of pie."

Now, he could see the pies in the case. But, she pointed at me and said, "The gentleman over there bought all of it."

Soon after that she came over to our table and said, "The gentleman over there would like to know if he can have a piece of pie."

"I don't know. What kind does he want?" He had apiece of pie and was not permitted to pay for it. It was our gift.

Others would come in and order pie and if I didn't like them they couldn't have a piece no matter how much they offered to pay.

I had become the Pie Baron!

I had cornered the market on pie.

After a couple of hours of this we sent the pies to a home for orphaned and abused children.

YOU GOTTA GRAB ANY ENJOYMENT YOU CAN IN LIFE, ANYWHERE AND ANYTIME YOU CAN.

JERE C.

Chapter 18

Why Can't We All Just Get Along?

Why can't we all just get along? Rodney King
The 12 & 12 says, "It is from our twisted relationships that we have suffered the most."

I was recently at a meeting when one of the women there was sharing. She had two sisters who didn't get along with each other. One of the sisters said, "If you have anything to do with the other sister, I will not speak to you." The other sister said the same thing! What was she supposed to do, make a choice?

We hear this kind of thing in the program a lot over and over.

Obviously, we come from dysfunctional families because we were members of them. If they had not been dysfunctional before we were born they would have become so because we were born. I came from a dysfunctional family. I created another dysfunctional family. The members of that family have created still other dysfunctional families.

I will probably be in even more trouble with members of my family because of what I have just written.

I thought when I stopped drinking everything would be OK. Most members of my family thought so, too.

As I sit writing these words, I am wearing a ring which my daughter, her husband, my son and his wife gave me on my 60th birthday. It has four small diamonds which represented the four "diamonds" in my life who gave it to me.

Today not one of those beautiful people even speaks to me, much less wants to be a part of my life. The advertisements say, "Diamonds are forever."

Claudette Colbert said, "Why do grandparents and grandchildren get along so well? They have the same enemy—the mother."

Was Ms Colbert right? I don't know. I don't think so. I hope not. But its clear that alcoholics do not hold the patent on dysfunctionalism.

Is there such a word as "disfunctionalism?" I hope so.

When I was living in Tampa, there were midnight meetings in my home group on Friday and Saturday. The most popular topic at those meetings was relationships." Can you imagine anything more insane than asking a bunch of people who have no place better to be at midnight on Friday or Saturday night for advice on relationships. And crazier yet, the folks there give each other the advice they seek!

I've been married four times, myself. Would you like to get your relationship advice from me? I look in the mirror and I think, "I'm not a woman, but if I were I'd be tickled to death to be married to him."

I still have my hair and my teeth and I leave the toilet seat down! Wow, I'm the answer to a maiden's prayer!

What more do they want? Evidently, they want more than that. Obviously, I just don't know what it is.

"Men marry women with the hope they will never change. Women marry men in the hope they will change. Invariably, both are disappointed." Albert Einstein

Two of the more popular topics at meetings of many groups are finance and romance. I can't even tell them apart.

"I have a way with women. It's a very expensive way, but what the hell, it's a way." Joey Adams

When I look back over those marriages, they all had one thing in common. Me.

"Always get married early in the morning. That way, if it doesn't work out, you haven't wasted a whole day." Micky Rooney

"The great question which has never been answered, and which I have never been able to answer, despite my 30 years of research into the feminine soul, is "What does a woman want?" Sigmund Freud

As you can easily tell from the above quotes, we are not the only people who have difficulty with relationships. We're just worse at it than most.

WHY CAN'T WE ALL JUST GET ALONG?

RODNEY KING

Chapter 19

Explain the Unexplainable

"If you wish to drown, do not torture yourself with shallow water." Russian Proverb

I think there comes a time in every alcoholics life when he is going to try to explain alcoholism to an earth person. I know I've tried it. And if you haven't yet, you probably will.

First of all, I don't understand how normal people drink. So why would I think I could explain how and why I drank?

I came home from college one weekend without telling anyone I was coming. There were several cars in the driveway.

I walked in the house without knocking, and saw my mother entertaining her bridge club. She and the "girls" were so embarrassed because I had caught them playing cards and drinking in the middle of the day! Oh, the shame of it! I walked out into the kitchen and there on the kitchen table was one miniature bottle. They had made four highballs out of it.

And they're out in the living room giggling, "Oh, my knees, they're all tingly."

Now, if you understand that kind of drinking, I have no idea why you are reading this book.

Another really fun thing to do is try to explain how AA works to a civilian. I know when I went to my first meeting, I thought the chairman owned the local franchise and at the end of the meeting they were going to sell me something. I thought it was some kind of multilevel sales deal. In a way it is, there's just no money in it.

Civilians will ask questions like, "Who's the president of AA or of the local group?"

"We don't have a president or even a vice-president."

"Well, who chairs the meetings?"

"We take turns."

"Then, who picks the chairman?"

"In our group its whoever, made the coffee."

"What about a treasurer? Surely you have a treasurer."

Yes, we do.

"Aren't you afraid the treasurer will take the group's treasury and get drunk?'

"It happens all the time. Mostly, we're afraid he'll be too embarrassed to come back. We don't want him to stay drunk or to stay away. Money is not the problem because we don't need much of that to run an AA group."

All across America there are probably a number of group treasurers right now out roaring drunk on a bender spending their groups treasury.

So, why does AA thrive and grow? I don't know. I guess its what many of us call a "God thing."

IF YOU WISH TO DROWN,

DO NOT TORTURE

YOURSELF WITH

SHALLOW WATER.

        RUSSIAN PROVERB

Chapter 20

Chippies

In my home group we have poker chips for those with less than one year of sobriety to mark their progress in the program. The poker chips, of various colors, are awarded at the close of the meetings to much applause and congratulations.

The poker chips have no mystical qualities. They are a reminder of what we are trying to do, to stay sober one day at a time. They are an effective reminder because they are bigger than any of the coins in your pocket or purse, which makes them just a little annoying.

Have you decided you want what we have and you're ready to go to any lengths to get it? Are you sick and tired of being sick and tired? Do you no longer wish to pay the high cost of low living? Have you relapsed and want to start over? Then you take a white poker chip.

Have you managed to go ninety days without a drink? Then you are eligible for the red poker chip. By this time, hopefully, you have a job, a prepaid cell phone, a buy here pay here car and contrary to your sponsors advice, a girl friend. Or if you are a woman, you have a boy friend who's moved in with you and can't or won't work and you're supporting him.

After six months you get your blue chip. By this time the buy here pay here car has quit running and the girl friend has dumped you, and hopefully you still have the job. Or if you are a woman, you still have the boy friend and the only way you're going to get rid of him is to move out yourself. Because he's not going anywhere.

After nine months you get the "much coveted gold" chip. Which is actually a white chip covered with gold spray paint. If you need to, you can scrape off the gold paint and see where you came from.

At the end of a year we give you a bronze medallion and throw a party in your honor with a birthday cake and people say a lot of mushy things about you and make you cry.

I remember early in my attempts at sobriety and I was a member of that subculture of AA that I call Slippers Monotonous. The maddest I ever got in an AA meeting was when one of the members was explaining the chips. He said, "We're all out of white chips. Al, can we use one of yours?"

I sure didn't appreciate that very much.

But, I gave him one.

If you think about it, considering all the pain that drinking has caused us, giving a bronze medallion to an alcoholic for not drinking is a little like giving one to a hemorrhoid sufferer for not going horseback riding.

"BEFORE YOU EMBARK UPON A JOURNEY OF REVENGE, DIG TWO GRAVES."

CONFUCIUS

Chapter 21

People Don't Act Right

It seems to me, that one of the popular topics raised at discussion meetings is what I call, "other people don't act right."

The raiser usually starts out, "My wife blah blah blah, my husband blah blah blah, my boss blah blah blah, my children blah blah blah, and so on ad infinitum.

In other words, someone isn't acting right and although the speaker never says so, what he really wants to know is, "How can I make them act right?" He already knows the answer to that. He knows he can't. But, that is what he really would like to know.

The fact is that other people don't act right. And what we need to learn is to accept that. They simply don't act right. They never have and they never will. And as Walter Cronkite used to say, "And that's the way it is."

I remember once, about twenty years ago a woman acted right for fifteen hours! Wow, that was wonderful. Unfortunately, she hasn't acted right since then.

There seems to be something about human nature that makes it easier to accept the behavior of others if we understand why they acted the way they did. I don't know why that helps, but somehow it does. So my little Nazi gave me a generic understanding. He asked me, "Do you know why some people act like horses asses?"

(You might want to underline or highlight this because its really heavy.)

He said, "Its because they ARE horses asses."

Isn't that wonderful? Isn't that simple?

There is a method you can use if you haven't reached the point of acceptance in your recovery.

You go tell another alcoholic all about what the other person did. Name names, dates, and places. Don't leave anything out. Then go to another alcoholic and do the same thing. Go to another alcoholic and do it again. Do it again. Somewhere about the fourth or fifth one you'll start into it and you'll say to yourself, "I don't even want to hear this again my self."

At that point it'll be pretty much over.

I didn't wind up in Alcoholics Anonymous because I was acting right. And then as soon as I got sober, I knew how everybody else ought to act. Isn't that amazing? Suddenly I was the world's leading authority on how everybody else ought to act.

No, I was in pain because of the gap between my standards and my behavior. I had coped with that pain by lowering my standards because I was unable to raise the level of my behavior. Eventually, I couldn't lower my standards fast enough and there really wasn't much left to do but get sober.

And the best place to do that was in Alcoholics Anonymous.

Today, to the best of my ability, I try to not pay any attention to what the others are doing. If I don't know what they are doing I'm not tempted to judge them.

I also have learned to accept the fact that many people think I don't act right. Surprise, surprise! The only difference being that I take a hard look to see if they might be right.

And then, some of them don't require any thought at all.

Most of us have at least one friend or family member who will tell us, "You're not really an alcoholic."

Another favorite is, "You go to too many meetings."

And the ever popular, "You've been sober a long time now don't you think you don't need those meetings any more?"

Sometimes the person, a devoutly religious Christian saying this is offended by AA references to "God as we understood Him." I usually ask, "Do you go to church?"

If he says he does, I ask him, "Have you been saved?"

If he says he has then I say, "Well then, you don't need to keep going there."

Here's a really weird one. "I don't think it's a good idea for you to hang around with those people."

Surely, you've heard, "Well, one drink isn't going to hurt you."

My grandson grew up very much like I did. By that I mean without friends his age, simply because of the location of his home. He used to call me and ask, "Grandpa, are you going to a meeting?"

I would nearly always say yes even if I hadn't planned on it. He wanted to go because he would meet his friends there and play with them during the meeting. Sometimes, if he liked the topic, he would sit in on an open meeting.

One individual, who shows signs of marijuana addiction, and has never been to a meeting tells me and others that taking my grandson with me to a meeting constituted child abuse. Is that stupid, or what?

How about, "You can have a beer because that's not really drinking."

I'm sure you can think of others.

All of the those people mean well. They are to be forgiven, but certainly not heeded.

Epilogue

I have not learned very much in AA, but I have unlearned a ton of stuff. I was not uneducated when I got sober. I knew a great deal, but most of what I knew wasn't so.

"We tried to hold on to our old ideas and the result was until we let go absolutely." Big Book of AA

It is obvious that my old ideas had not worked, because if they had, I would not have needed AA and I would not have needed alcohol in the first place. I would simply have lived happily ever after with no need for alcohol, meetings, steps or any of that other stuff.

While writing this little book I kept asking myself if I have been walking the walk I have been talking. If I have, it's only because God has walked it with me. And not because of any abilities of mine.

Over the last three years I was in a slip and fall type accident for which I now have a titanium tie rod and ball joint in my arm and shoulder. And I laughed. I could have gotten the same hardware at Discount Auto Parts for a whole lot less.

I developed colon cancer, the surgeon turned my colon into a semi-colon, they put me on radiation and chemotherapy. And I laughed. I went through a financially disastrous marriage and divorce. And I laughed.

A beloved family member "went back out" on alcohol and crack cocaine, and stole tens of thousands of dollars from me. And I laughed.

I didn't laugh because I enjoyed any of those events. I would have much preferred none of them had ever happened. I laughed because God has insulated me from the pain I previously would have felt. To me, that's what the Big Book means when it promises "a new freedom and a new happiness."

The compliment I treasure more than any others came from Nicky Lee (Probably not his real name) and was not intended as a compliment at all. He was going through difficulties of his own at the same time as mine and in a meeting said, "Al, it's easy for you. All you have to worry about is where you're going to pee."

Today I remember back to when I first joined the fellowship and I saw old timers going through terrible tragedies with an obvious serenity. I remember thinking about what thick skinned hard hearted sons of bitches they were. But they were nothing like that. They were caring, sharing teddy bears.

Instead of feeling sorry for themselves, They dealt with their feelings by working with others.

There once was a very wise old man who lived in the ancient town of Athens, Greece. His name was Socrates. So great was this man's reputation for wisdom, judgement and knowledge, that men came from every corner of the known civilized world to sit at his feet, to listen and learn. Men of no less stature than Plato himself.

There were two young men in Athens who became jealous of the accolades being paid this great and wise old man. They went up into the hills surrounding the city and caught a sparrow. They returned to Athens and approached Socrates.

With one of them hiding the sparrow in his hands, he asked, "Tell us, what I have in my hands."

Socrates could see part of it's tail feathers and replied, "It is probably a sparrow."

"That's correct! Now if you really are as intelligent and wise as people say you are, tell us if the sparrow is dead or alive."

And Socrates answered, "Its in your hands."

"What kind of an answer is that?"

"You are probably holding that sparrow with its neck lodged between your thumb and forefinger. If I say the sparrow is alive, you'll snap it's neck, open your hands and the sparrow will be dead. If, on the other hand, I say the sparrow is dead, you will open your hands and the sparrow will soar into the heavens."

Your life is in your hands. It is my sincere prayer that you will be able to open those hands, place your will and your life in His care and let your future soar into the heavens or to whatever heights you wish.

May God bless you.

Broccoli Al

Made in the USA
Charleston, SC
09 June 2010